Deb
SAVES THE DAY

The story of Deborah
Judges 4–5 for children

Written by Erik Rottmann
Illustrated by Stephen Marchesi

CONCORDIA PUBLISHING HOUSE · SAINT LOUIS

God gave His people Israel
A rich and promised land.
But not long after they moved in,
Their troubles sure began.

Their hearts grew cold and soon they all
Did evil in God's sight.
God handed them to Sisera,
A cruel Canaanite.

Sisera had iron strength.
He led for twenty years.
His army and his chariots
Moved Israel to tears.

Deborah came in answer to
The people's prayer to God.
She came to conquer Sisera;
To break his cruel rod.

Barak was a mighty man,
But he felt too afraid
To fight against the Canaanite.
So Deborah gave him aid.

She said to Barak, "Go to war!
No longer quake with fear!
If you can't fight him on your own,
You will have me near."

"I will be right by your side.
God gives the victory.
Sisera shall lose his life
To someone just like me."

So Deborah strengthened Barak's heart.
His courage grew inside.
They went to war with Sisera.
They chased him side-by-side.

While Sisera was on the run
From Deborah and her quest,
He stopped to hide in Jael's tent
Because he needed rest.

Jael let him fall asleep, but
Not for very long.
She killed the man whom Deborah sought.
Then Deborah sang this song:

"God raised for us in Israel
Someone to lead the way
To fight against our enemies
And finally win the day!"

"Give ear, O princes! Listen, kings!
To God above I sing!
Because the Lord gives victory,
Let all His praises ring!"

Through Deborah, God gave strength and faith
In Barak's time of doubt.
God also does the same for you!
You'll never go without!

God gave to you the Christ, your Lord,
Forgiving all your sins.
He also gives you strength and faith
And brand-new life within.

God sends you people in your life
To comfort you with care;
To walk with you and talk with you,
Or simply just be there.

God also sends His angels out
To bear you on your way;
To guard you and watch over you
As Deborah did that day.

Dear Parents,

Like the adults around them, children often experience deep feelings of fear and uncertainty. Their fears may be the result of real events (such as a traumatic experience) or imagined dangers (such as the monster under the bed).

Through the death and resurrection of His Son Jesus Christ, God the Father gives to us His great gifts of forgiveness, life, and salvation. God loves us so greatly that He lavishes upon us many other gifts as well. Among these, He gives us peace of mind and freedom from fear. This freedom from fear is rooted in our Lord's divine promise, "I am with you always" (Matthew 28:20).

Use this story of Deborah as a way of teaching your child that God's loving promises will give her comfort when she feels afraid. Explain to her that, just as Deborah comforted and encouraged Barak, so also does God give us many things for our comfort and peace. These include parents, grandparents, friends, angels, and so on. You could also point out to your child these other passages from God's powerful Word that promise freedom from fear:

"The Lord is my shepherd; . . .
I will fear no evil."
Psalm 23:1, 4

"If God is for us, who can be against us?"
Romans 8:31

"I will never leave you nor forsake you."
Hebrews 13:5

The Author